Published 2024

FiNGERPRINT!

An imprint of **Prakash Books India Pvt. Ltd**

113/A, Darya Ganj,
New Delhi-110 002
Email: info@prakashbooks.com/sales@prakashbooks.com

⬛ Fingerprint Publishing
❎ @FingerprintP
⭕ @fingerprintpublishingbooks

ISBN: 978 93 5856 829 5

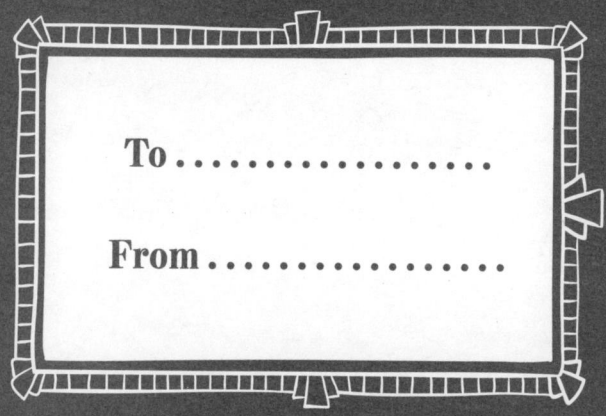

To . . . .

From . . . .

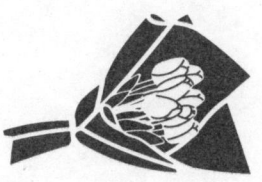

Kindness is not just a virtue, it's a superpower.
It can melt the coldest hearts, heal the deepest
wounds, brighten the darkest days, and leave
a lasting impact on those we encounter.

But kindness is not always easy. Sometimes,
it's hard to be kind when you're tired, stressed,
angry, or dealing with bullies. But that's
when kindness matters the most. That's when
kindness can make a difference. That's when
kindness can save the day. So don't be a jerk,
be a hero.

Shine as a guiding light that reignites someone's
faith in humanity, one act of kindness at a time.

"The only way to tell the truth
is to speak with kindness.
Only the words of a loving
man can be heard."

HENRY DAVID
THOREAU

"KINDNESS IS THE GREATEST STRENGTH ONE CAN POSSESS."

Anonymous

"My religion is very simple.
My religion is kindness."

14ᵀᴴ DALAI LAMA

"Carry out a random act of kindness, with no expectation of reward, safe in the knowledge that one day someone might do the same for you."

PRINCESS DIANA

"The fragrance always remains in the hand that gives the rose."

HEDA BEJAR

"Kindness is the language
which the deaf can hear
and the blind can see."

MARK TWAIN

"KINDNESS IS THE SUNSHINE IN WHICH VIRTUE GROWS."

Robert Green Ingersoll

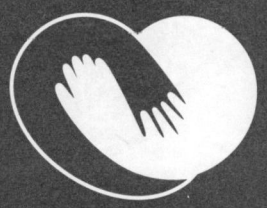

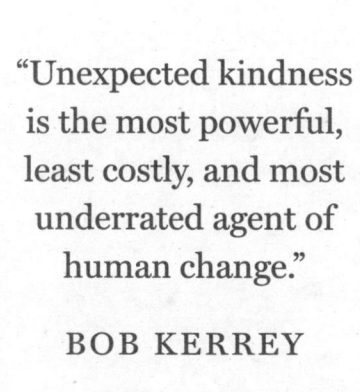

"Unexpected kindness
is the most powerful,
least costly, and most
underrated agent of
human change."

BOB KERREY

"Authenticity, living your truth, kindness—these are necessary virtues."

MERLE DANDRIDGE

"Nothing is black or white, nothing's 'us or them.' But then there are magical, beautiful things in the world. There's incredible acts of kindness and bravery, and in the most unlikely places, and it gives you hope."

DAVE MATTHEWS

"LOVE AND KINDNESS
ARE NEVER WASTED.
THEY ALWAYS MAKE
A DIFFERENCE."

Helen James

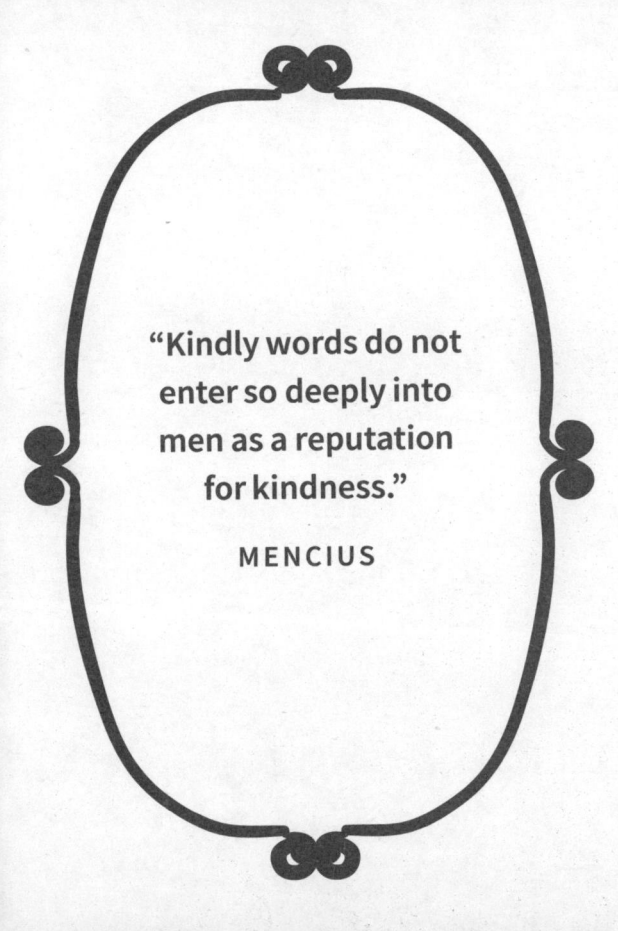

"Kindly words do not
enter so deeply into
men as a reputation
for kindness."

MENCIUS

"Do small things with great love."

MOTHER TERESA

"YOU WILL NEVER
REGRET BEING KIND."

Nicole Shepherd

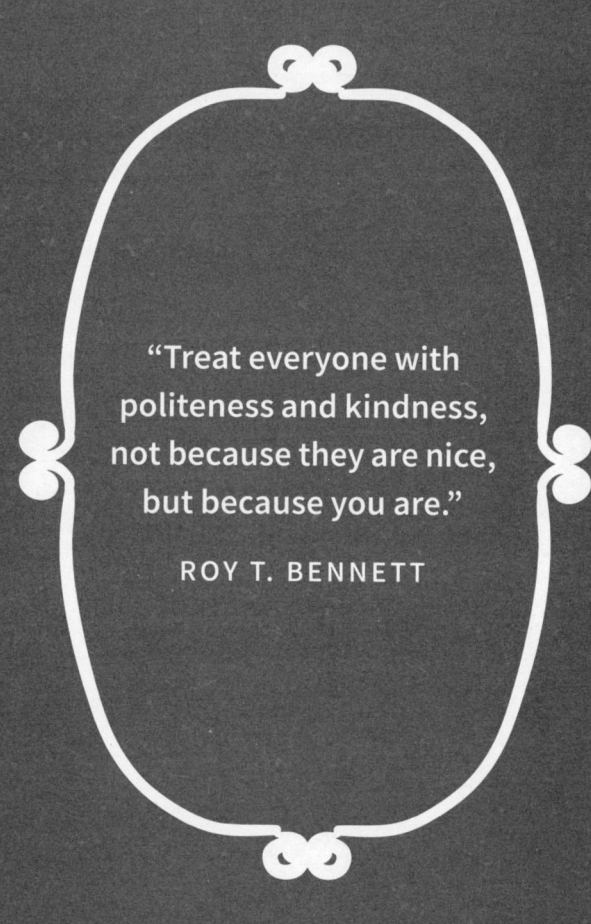

"Treat everyone with politeness and kindness, not because they are nice, but because you are."

ROY T. BENNETT

"Kindness is the language of love."

DEBASISH MRIDHA

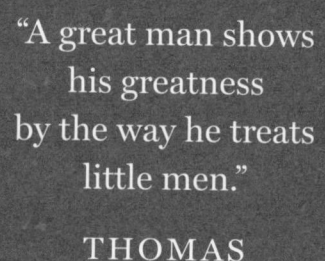

"A great man shows
his greatness
by the way he treats
little men."

THOMAS
CARLYLE

"The catch phrase for the day is 'Do an act of kindness. Help one person smile.'"

HARVEY BALL

"Remember, there's no
such thing as a small act
of kindness. Every act creates
a ripple with no logical end."

SCOTT ADAMS

"You cannot do a kindness too soon because you never know how soon it will be too late."

RALPH WALDO EMERSON

"We can each change
the world, with genuine
acts of kindness."

MONGAI FANKAM

"A SINGLE ACT OF KINDNESS THROWS OUT ROOTS IN ALL DIRECTIONS, AND THE ROOTS SPRING UP AND MAKE NEW TREES."

Amelia Earhart

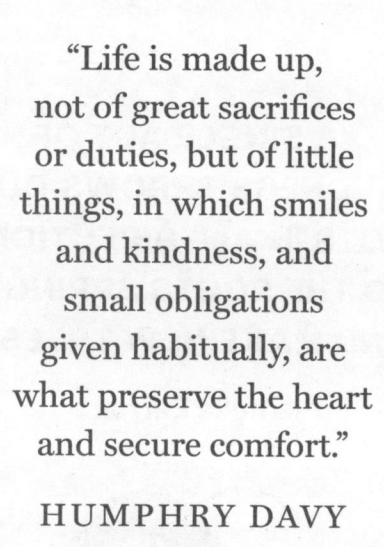

"Life is made up,
not of great sacrifices
or duties, but of little
things, in which smiles
and kindness, and
small obligations
given habitually, are
what preserve the heart
and secure comfort."

HUMPHRY DAVY

"THE TRUE MEASURE OF
A MAN IS HOW HE TREATS
SOMEONE WHO CAN DO HIM
ABSOLUTELY NO GOOD."

Samuel Johnson

"In the vast universe of human interaction, kindness is the constellation that connects us all, creating a celestial map of compassion that guides our journey through life."

A.D. Posey

"Empathy is choosing to see ourselves in another despite our differences. It's recognizing that the same humanity—the same desire for meaning, fulfillment and security—exists in each of us, even if it's expressed uniquely."

VIVEK MURTHY

"THE SMALLEST ACT OF KINDNESS IS WORTH MORE THAN THE GRANDEST INTENTION."

Oscar Wilde

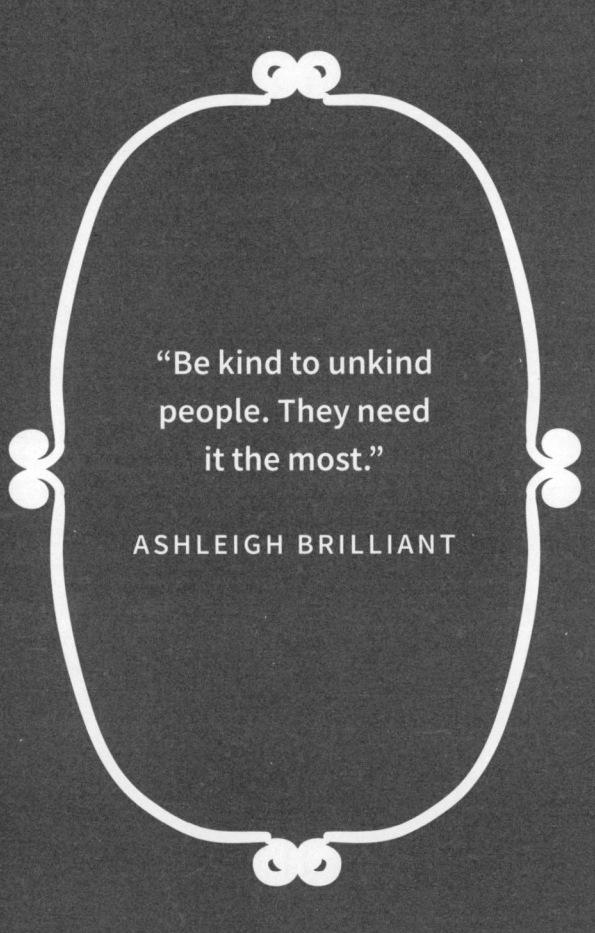

"Be kind to unkind
people. They need
it the most."

ASHLEIGH BRILLIANT

"When words are both
true and kind, they can
change the world."

BUDDHA

"BEING KIND IS NOT A RANDOM ACT; IT'S A DELIBERATE CHOICE TO SPRINKLE THE WORLD WITH THE STARDUST OF GOODNESS."

Amy Leigh Mercree

"No act of kindness, no matter
how small, is ever wasted."

AESOP

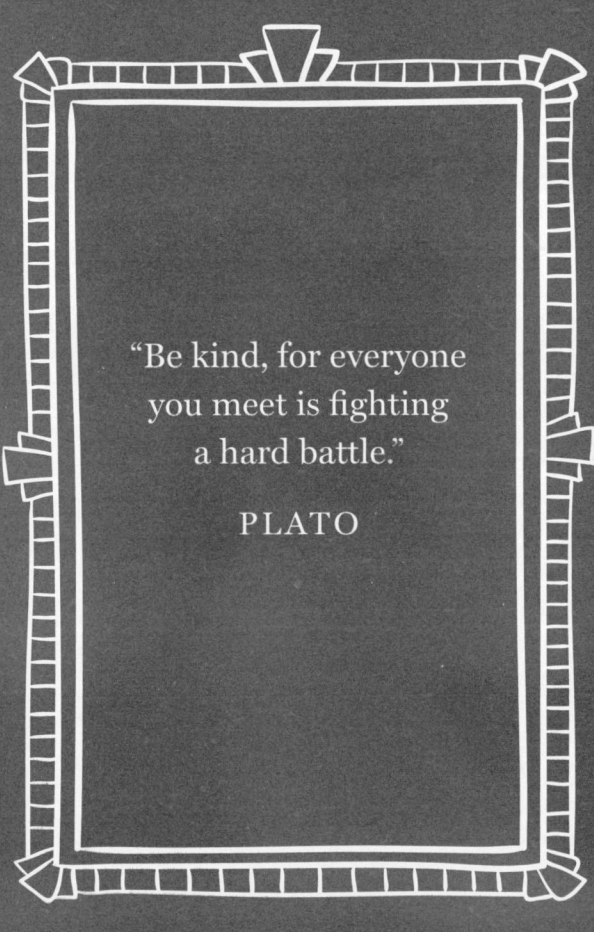

"Be kind, for everyone
you meet is fighting
a hard battle."

PLATO

"A kind word is like
a spring day."

RUSSIAN PROVERB

"The true meaning of life is
to plant trees under whose
shade you do not expect to sit."

NELSON HENDERSON

"YOUR ACTS OF KINDNESS ARE
IRIDESCENT WINGS OF DIVINE
LOVE, WHICH LINGER AND
CONTINUE TO UPLIFT OTHERS
LONG AFTER YOUR SHARING."

Rumi

"KINDNESS IS THE LIGHT
THAT DISSOLVES ALL
WALLS BETWEEN SOULS,
FAMILIES, AND NATIONS."

Paramahansa Yogananda

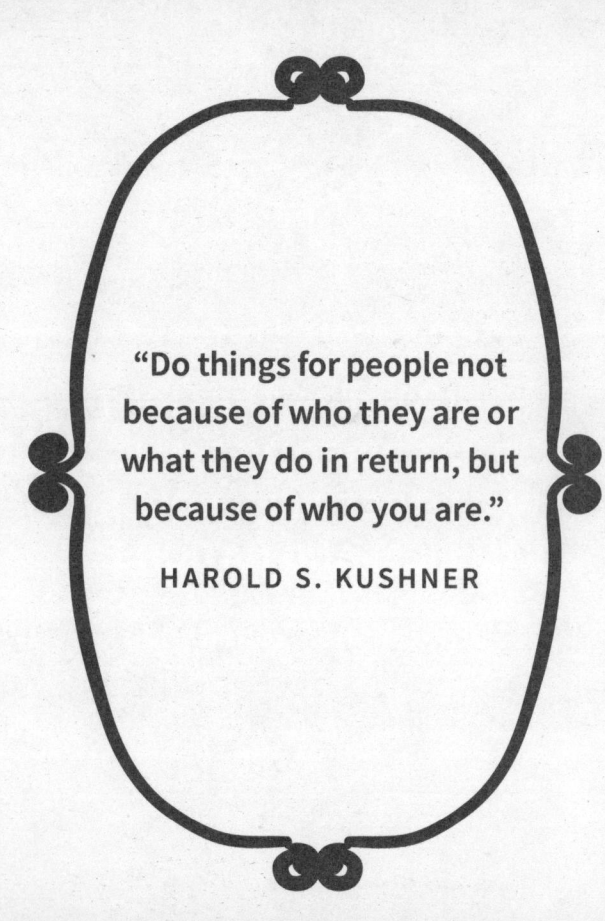

"Do things for people not because of who they are or what they do in return, but because of who you are."

HAROLD S. KUSHNER

"Kindness is the best form of humanity."

DORIS LEE MCCOY

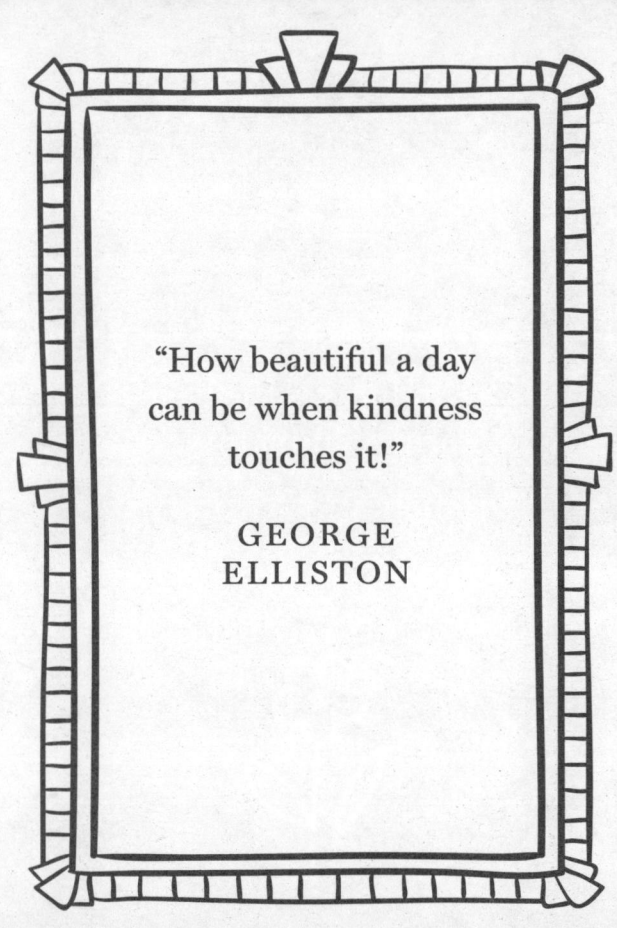

"How beautiful a day
can be when kindness
touches it!"

GEORGE
ELLISTON

"A part of kindness consists in loving people more than they deserve."

JOSEPH JOUBERT

"Compassion isn't about
solutions. It's about giving
all the love that you've got."

CHERYL STRAYED

WHY IS IT IMPORTANT TO BE KIND?

❀ When you approach people with kindness, empathy, and respect, it fosters positive connections and relationships.

❀ It creates a ripple effect of positivity. When you are kind to someone, they are likely to show kindness to others.

❀ It encourages empathy by allowing you to put yourself in someone else's shoes and understand their perspective.

❀ Kindness makes an impact, no matter how small the gesture. It can brighten someone's day and provide much-needed support.

"Kindness is the bridge
between all people."

ANONYMOUS

"I think probably kindness is my number one attribute in a human being. I'll put it before any of the things like courage or bravery or generosity or anything else."

ROALD DAHL

"SPREAD LOVE EVERYWHERE YOU GO. LET NO ONE EVER COME TO YOU WITHOUT LEAVING HAPPIER."

Mother Teresa

"KINDNESS IS THE UNIVERSAL LANGUAGE THAT TRANSCENDS BORDERS, CULTURES, AND DIFFERENCES."

Jacqueline Winspear

"For attractive lips, speak words of kindness. For lovely eyes, seek out the good in people. For a slim figure, share your food with the hungry. For beautiful hair, let a child run his fingers through it once a day. For poise, walk with the knowledge that you will never walk alone."

SAM LEVENSON

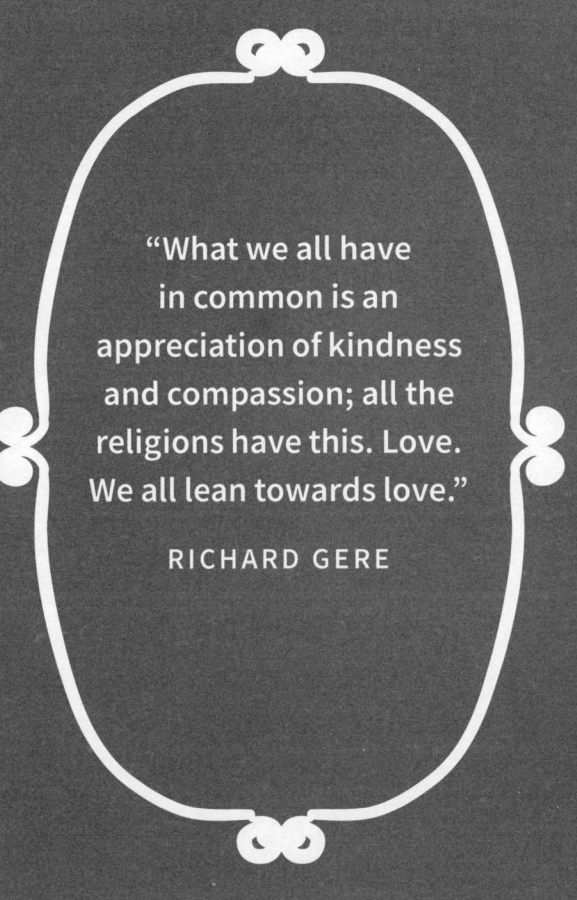

"What we all have
in common is an
appreciation of kindness
and compassion; all the
religions have this. Love.
We all lean towards love."

RICHARD GERE

"HUMAN KINDNESS HAS NEVER WEAKENED THE STAMINA OR SOFTENED THE FIBER OF A FREE PEOPLE."

Franklin D. Roosevelt

"That is what compassion does. It challenges our assumptions, our sense of self-limitation, worthlessness, of not having a place in the world, our feelings of loneliness and estrangement. These are narrow, constrictive states of mind. As we develop compassion, our hearts open."

SHARON SALZBERG

"Kindness can become
its own motive. We are
made kind by being kind."

ERIC HOFFER

"WHEN YOU CALLOUSLY IGNORE THE SUFFERING OF OTHERS, YOU LOSE THE CAPACITY TO SHARE THEIR HAPPINESS, TOO."

Albert Schweitzer

"Practice random
kindness and senseless
acts of beauty."

ANNE HERBERT

"A kind gesture can reach a wound that only compassion can heal."

STEVE MARABOLI

"ALWAYS BE A LITTLE KINDER THAN NECESSARY."

James M. Barrie

"WHAT WISDOM CAN YOU
FIND THAT IS GREATER
THAN KINDNESS?"

Jean-Jacques Rousseau

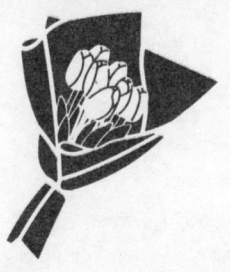

"Never doubt that a small group
of thoughtful, committed citizens
can change the world. Indeed,
it is the only thing that ever has."

MARGARET MEAD

"Kindness is the only service that will stand the storm of life and not wash out. It will wear well and will be remembered long after the prism of politeness or the complexion of courtesy has faded away."

ABRAHAM LINCOLN

"Do your little bit of good where you are; it's those little bits of good put together that overwhelm the world."

DESMOND TUTU

"TO ERR ON THE SIDE OF KINDNESS IS SELDOM AN ERROR."

Liz Armbruster

"My wish for you is that you continue. Continue to be who and how you are, to astonish a mean world with your acts of kindness. Continue to allow humor to lighten the burden of your tender heart."

MAYA ANGELOU

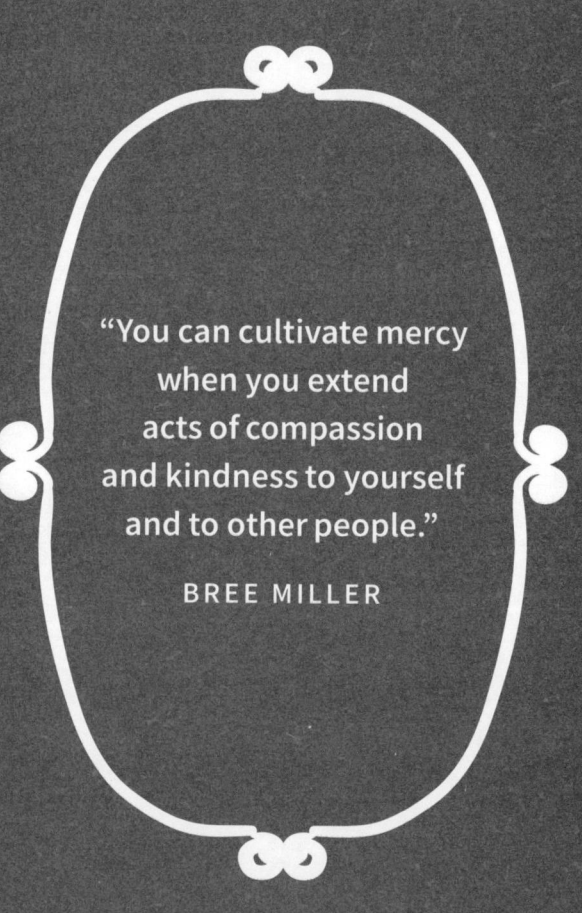

"You can cultivate mercy
when you extend
acts of compassion
and kindness to yourself
and to other people."

BREE MILLER

"Kindness is an electrical spark of life that runs through all kingdoms and has a reciprocal action when shown to others."

JOE HAYES

"IT IS THE CHARACTERISTIC
OF THE MAGNANIMOUS
MAN TO ASK NO FAVOR
BUT TO BE READY TO DO
KINDNESS TO OTHERS."

Aristotle

"KINDNESS IS THE COMPASS
THAT POINTS US IN THE
DIRECTION OF OUR
SHARED HUMANITY."

Piero Ferrucci

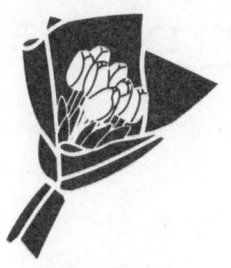

"Sometimes it takes only one
act of kindness and caring
to change a person's life."

JACKIE CHAN

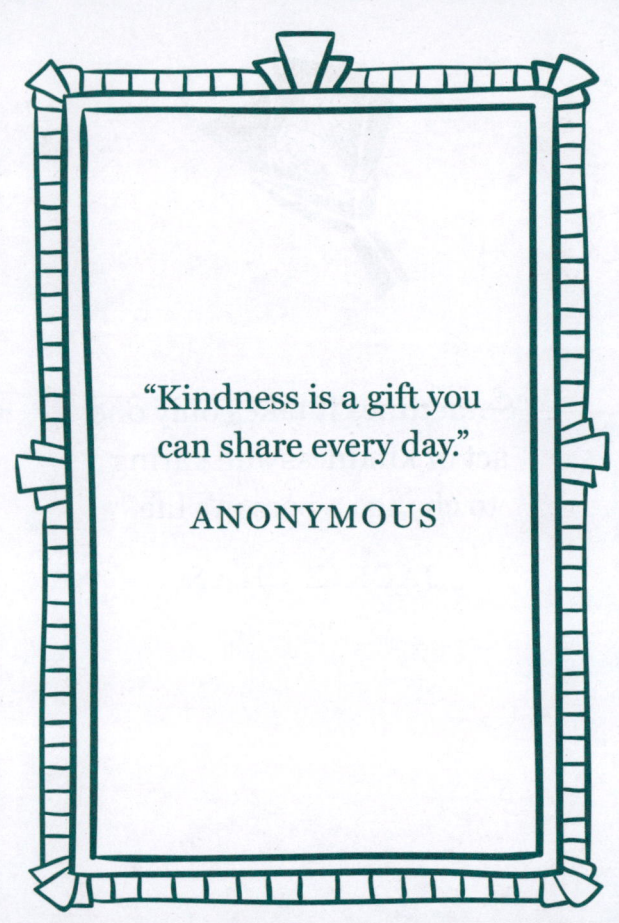

"Kindness is a gift you
can share every day."

ANONYMOUS

"Because that's what kindness is. It's not doing something for someone else because they can't, but because you can."

ANDREW ISKANDER

"Guard well within yourself that treasure, kindness. Know how to give without hesitation, how to lose without regret, how to acquire without meanness."

GEORGE SAND

"Kindness begins
with the understanding
that we all struggle."

CHARLES GLASSMAN

"The words of kindness are more healing to a drooping heart than balm or honey."

SARAH FIELDING

"Wherever there is a
human being, there is an
opportunity for a kindness."

LUCIUS ANNAEUS SENECA

"TO PRACTICE FIVE THINGS UNDER ALL CIRCUMSTANCES CONSTITUTES PERFECT VIRTUE; THESE FIVE ARE GRAVITY, GENEROSITY OF SOUL, SINCERITY, EARNESTNESS, AND KINDNESS."

Confucius

"KINDNESS AND
POLITENESS ARE NOT
OVERRATED AT ALL.
THEY'RE UNDERUSED."

Tommy Lee Jones

"You can accomplish
by kindness what
you cannot by force."

PUBLILIUS SYRUS

"SIMPLE KINDNESS MAY BE THE MOST VITAL KEY TO THE RIDDLE OF HOW HUMAN BEINGS CAN LIVE WITH EACH OTHER IN PEACE AND CARE PROPERLY FOR THIS PLANET WE ALL SHARE."

Bo Lozoff

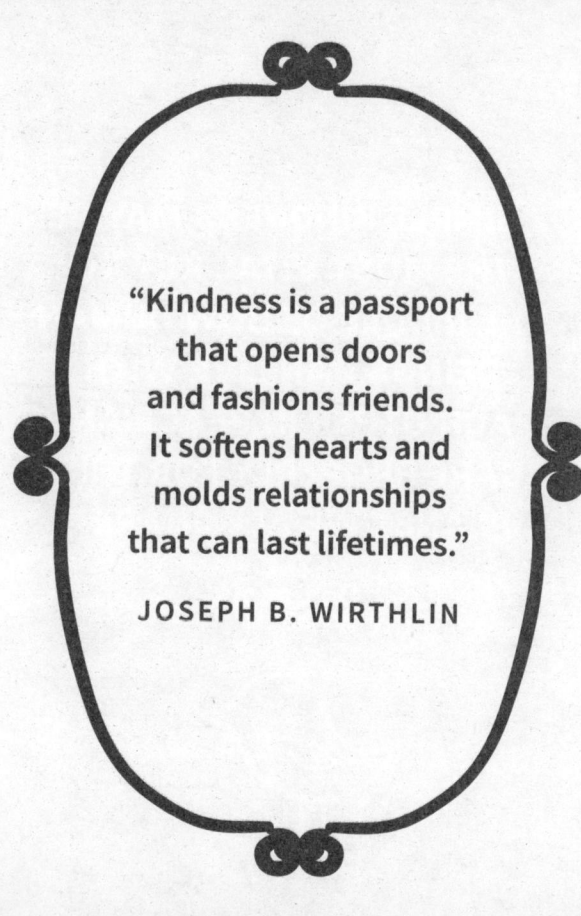

"Kindness is a passport
that opens doors
and fashions friends.
It softens hearts and
molds relationships
that can last lifetimes."

JOSEPH B. WIRTHLIN

"Too often we underestimate the power of a touch, a smile, a kind word, a listening ear, an honest compliment, or the smallest act of caring, all of which have the potential to turn a life around."

LEO BUSCAGLIA

"HOW DO WE CHANGE THE
WORLD? ONE RANDOM ACT
OF KINDNESS AT A TIME."

Morgan Freeman

"When I was young, I admired clever people. Now that I am old, I admire kind people."

ABRAHAM
JOSHUA HESCHEL

"Never look down on anybody unless you're helping them up."

JESSE JACKSON

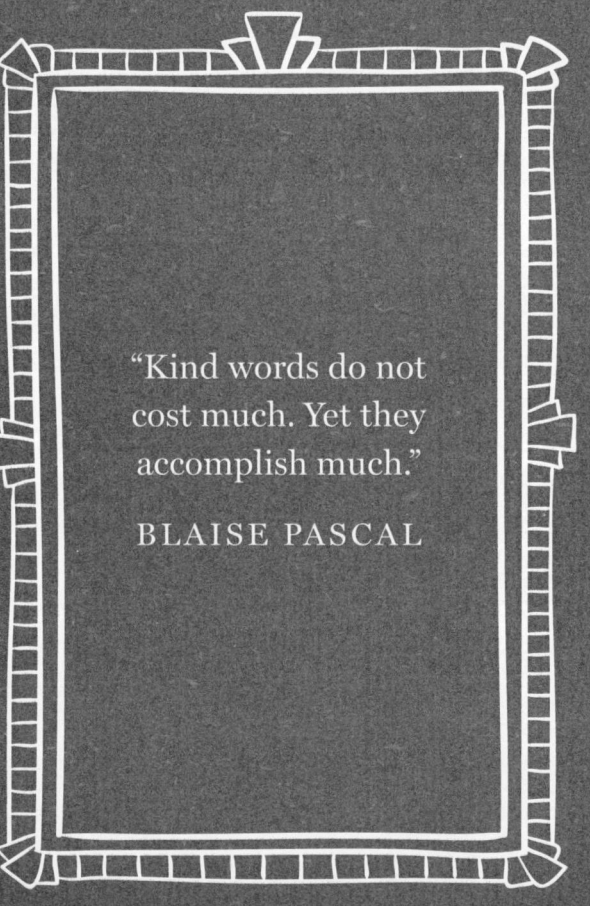

"Kind words do not cost much. Yet they accomplish much."

BLAISE PASCAL

"Kindness is the gentle echo of a compassionate soul, reverberating through the corridors of time."

R.J. PALACIO

"A LITTLE THOUGHT AND A LITTLE KINDNESS ARE OFTEN WORTH MORE THAN A GREAT DEAL OF MONEY."

John Ruskin

"Kindness gives
birth to kindness."

SOPHOCLES

"Kindness is more important than wisdom, and the recognition of this is the beginning of wisdom."

THEODORE ISAAC RUBIN

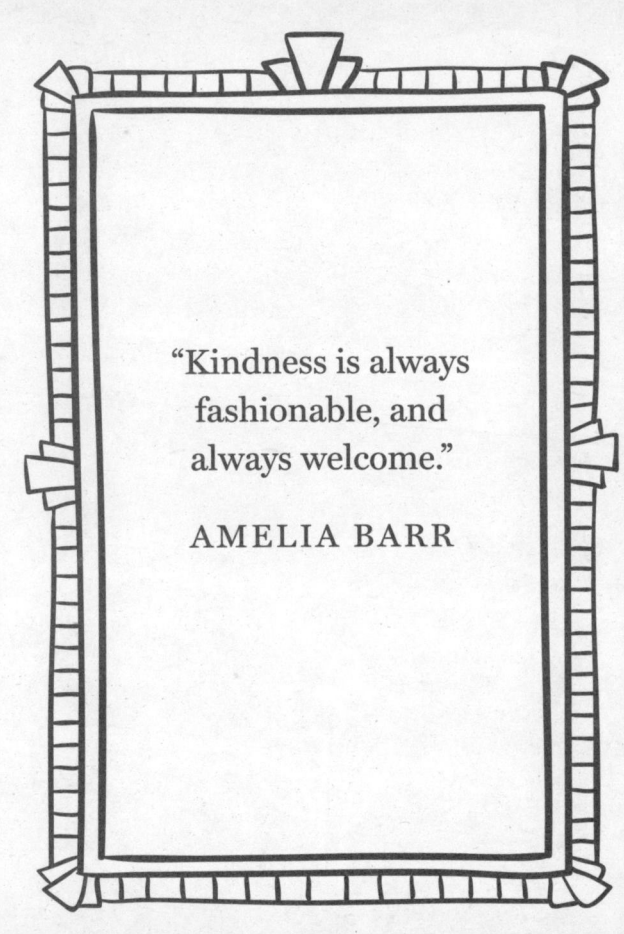

"Kindness is always
fashionable, and
always welcome."

AMELIA BARR

"Kindness in words
creates confidence.
Kindness in thinking
creates profoundness.
Kindness in giving
creates love."

LAO TZU

"Three things in human
life are important.
The first is to be kind.
The second is to be kind.
And the third is to
be kind."

HENRY JAMES

"WHATEVER POSSESSION
WE GAIN BY OUR SWORD
CANNOT BE SURE OR
LASTING, BUT THE LOVE
GAINED BY KINDNESS
AND MODERATION IS
CERTAIN AND DURABLE."

Alexander the Great

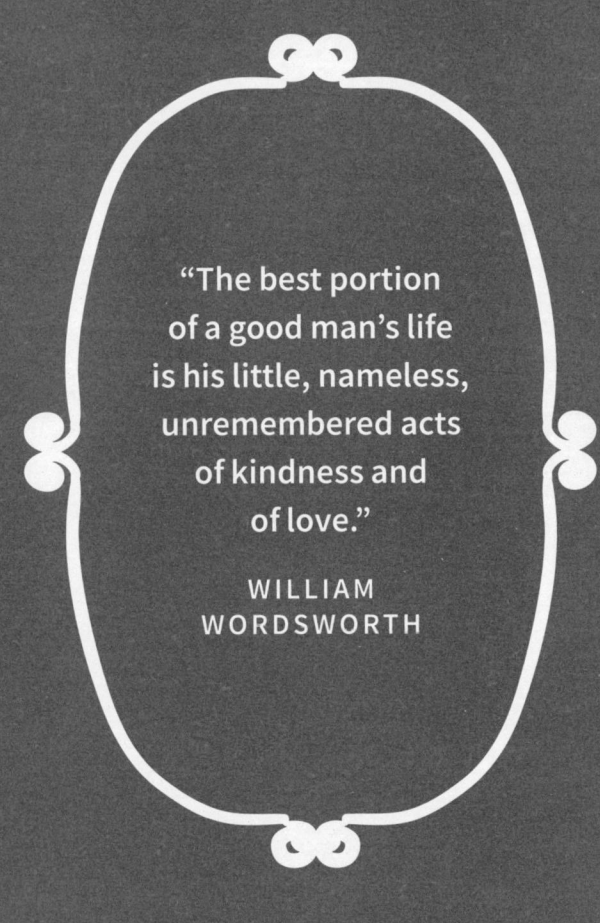

"The best portion
of a good man's life
is his little, nameless,
unremembered acts
of kindness and
of love."

WILLIAM
WORDSWORTH

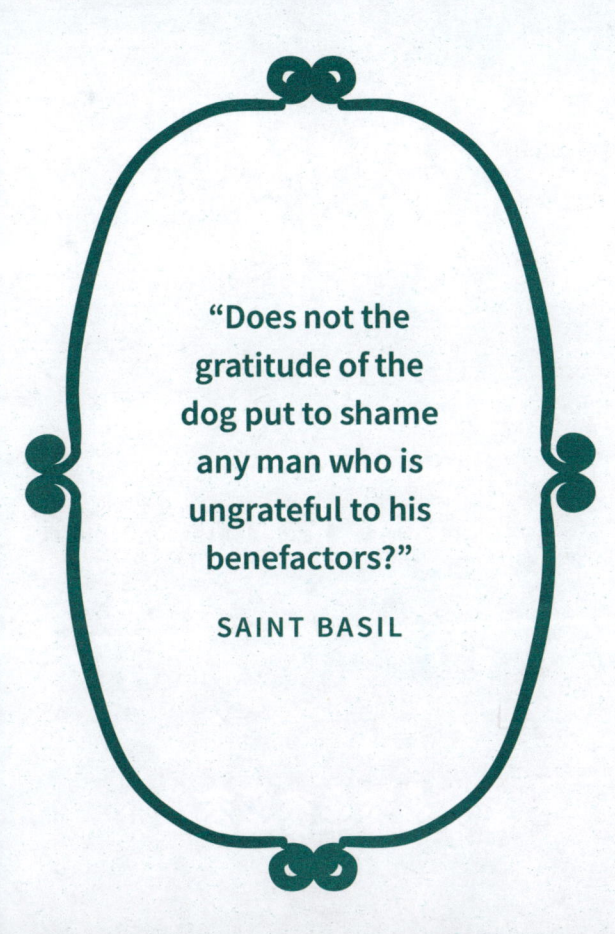

"Does not the gratitude of the dog put to shame any man who is ungrateful to his benefactors?"

SAINT BASIL

"A warm smile is the universal language of kindness."

WILLIAM ARTHUR WARD

"In a gentle way, you
can shake the world."

MAHATMA GANDHI

"Kindness is a reflection
of inner strength."

ANONYMOUS

"EVERY DAY, SOME ACT OF KINDNESS COMES MY WAY, EVEN IF IT'S JUST SOMEONE OPENING THE DOOR. IT HAPPENS EVERY DAY IF YOU KEEP AN EYE OUT FOR IT. KEEPING AN EYE OUT, THAT'S THE KEY."

Aaron Neville

"Real generosity
is doing something
nice for someone who
will never find out."

FRANK A.
CLARK

"The only way to deal with fear is to face it head-on. When you show fear kindness and love, it will melt away."

NIKKI ROWE

"Kindness is the investment that pays the highest returns."

ROSEMARY ELLEN GUILEY

"FOR BEAUTIFUL EYES, LOOK FOR THE GOOD IN OTHERS; FOR BEAUTIFUL LIPS, SPEAK ONLY WORDS OF KINDNESS; AND FOR POISE, WALK WITH THE KNOWLEDGE THAT YOU ARE NEVER ALONE."

Audrey Hepburn

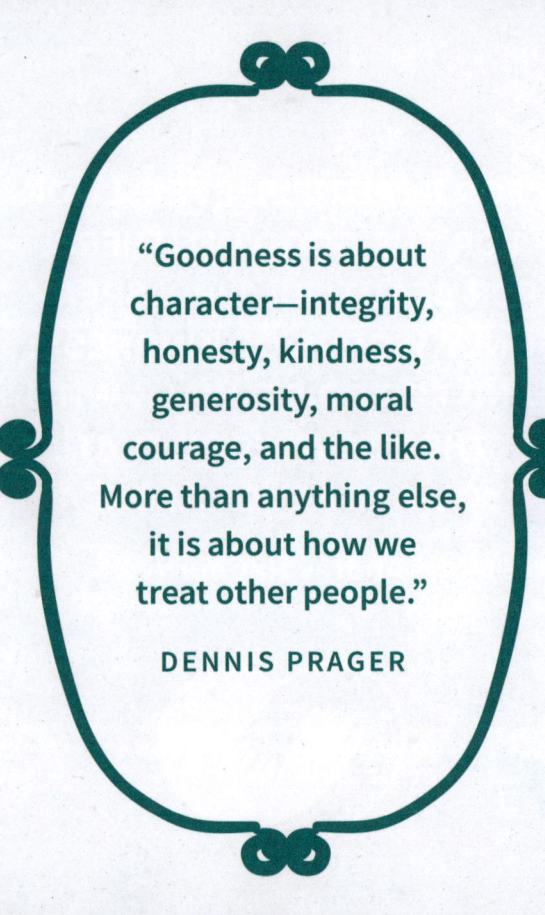

"Goodness is about character—integrity, honesty, kindness, generosity, moral courage, and the like. More than anything else, it is about how we treat other people."

DENNIS PRAGER

"Beginning today, treat
everyone you meet as if they
were going to be dead by
midnight. Extend to them
all the care, kindness and
understanding you can muster,
and do it with no thought
of any reward. Your life will
never be the same again."

OG MANDINO

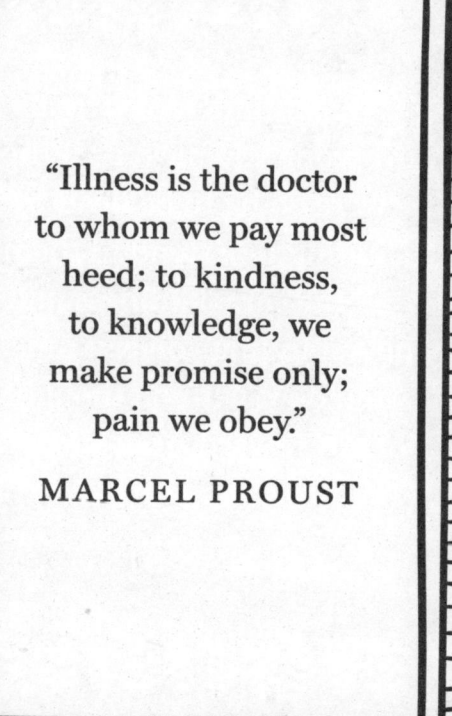

"Illness is the doctor
to whom we pay most
heed; to kindness,
to knowledge, we
make promise only;
pain we obey."

MARCEL PROUST

"Together we can make a difference just one act of kindness at a time."

RON HALL

"Kindness is the
music the heart sings."

ANONYMOUS

LITTLE ACTS OF KINDNESS THAT CAN MAKE A BIG DIFFERENCE!

❀ Whether it's helping someone with heavy bags or helping a stranger in need, your small act of kindness can inspire people.

❀ Take the time to listen to someone. It will give them a safe space to express themselves.

❀ Write a heartfelt note to someone. It shows that you care enough to go the extra mile, and they can revisit your kind words whenever they need them.

❀ Be kind to yourself. It encourages self-acceptance, boosts self-esteem, and reduces stress.

❀ Read books. It fosters empathy by allowing you to immerse yourself in diverse characters' perspectives and experiences.

"Kindness, I've discovered,
is everything in life."

ISAAC BASHEVIS SINGER

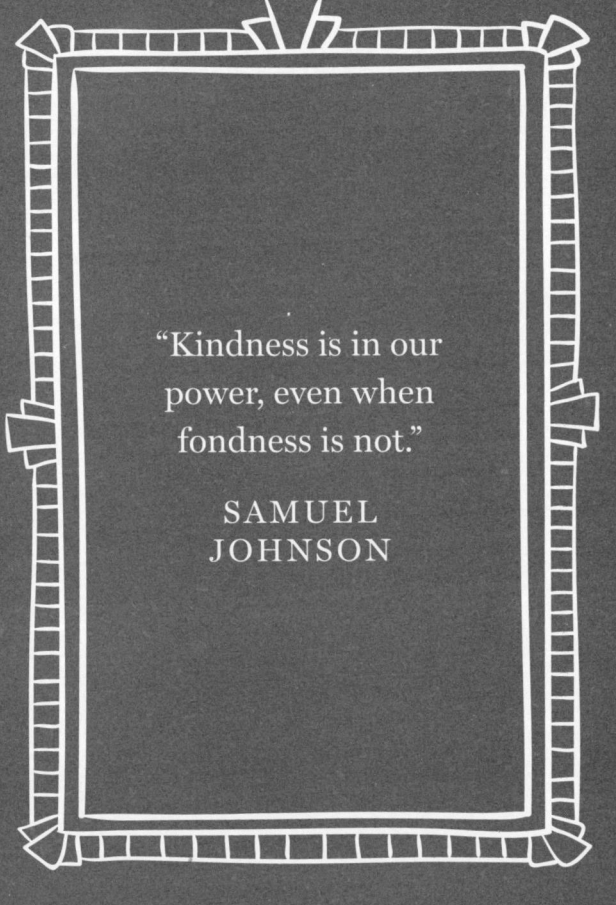

"Kindness is in our power, even when fondness is not."

SAMUEL
JOHNSON

"YOU CAN BE RICH IN
SPIRIT, KINDNESS, LOVE
AND ALL THOSE THINGS
THAT YOU CAN'T PUT
A DOLLAR SIGN ON."

Dolly Parton

"With all of the bad things that are happening in the world right now, I think we need a message of togetherness and true unity. I believe that starts with personal reflection and then we can find kindness toward each other."

MARIELLE HELLER

"It's not our job to play judge and jury, to determine who is worthy of our kindness and who is not. We just need to be kind, unconditionally and without ulterior motive, even—or rather, especially—when we'd prefer not to be."

JOSH RADNOR

"WHEN THE NORM IS DECENCY, OTHER VIRTUES CAN THRIVE: INTEGRITY, HONESTY, COMPASSION, KINDNESS, AND TRUST."

Raja Krishnamoorthi

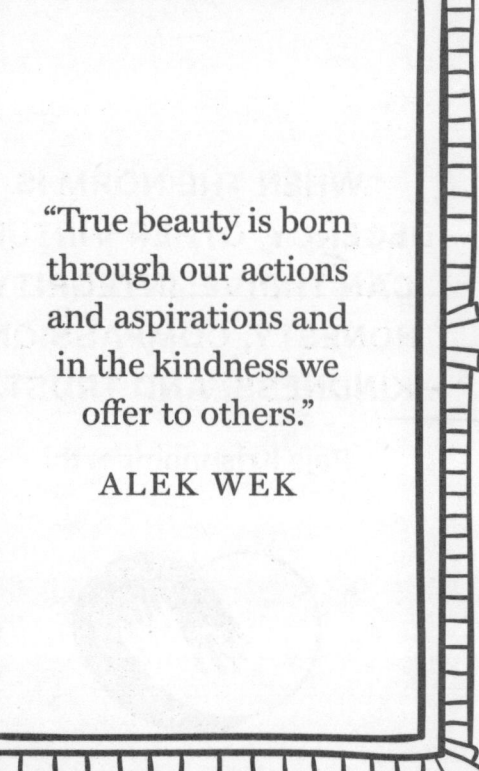

"True beauty is born through our actions and aspirations and in the kindness we offer to others."

ALEK WEK

"ASK YOURSELF: HAVE YOU BEEN KIND TODAY? MAKE KINDNESS YOUR DAILY MODUS OPERANDI AND CHANGE YOUR WORLD."

Annie Lennox

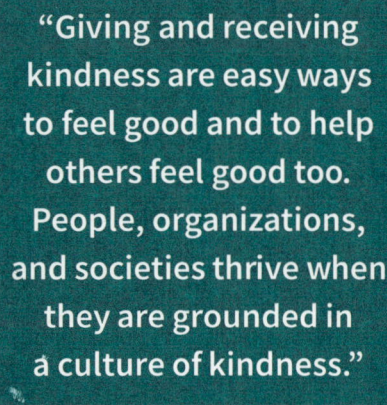

"Giving and receiving
kindness are easy ways
to feel good and to help
others feel good too.
People, organizations,
and societies thrive when
they are grounded in
a culture of kindness."

VIVEK MURTHY

"Every minute of every
hour of every day you are
making the world, just as
you are making yourself,
and you might as well
do it with generosity
and kindness and style."

REBECCA SOLNIT

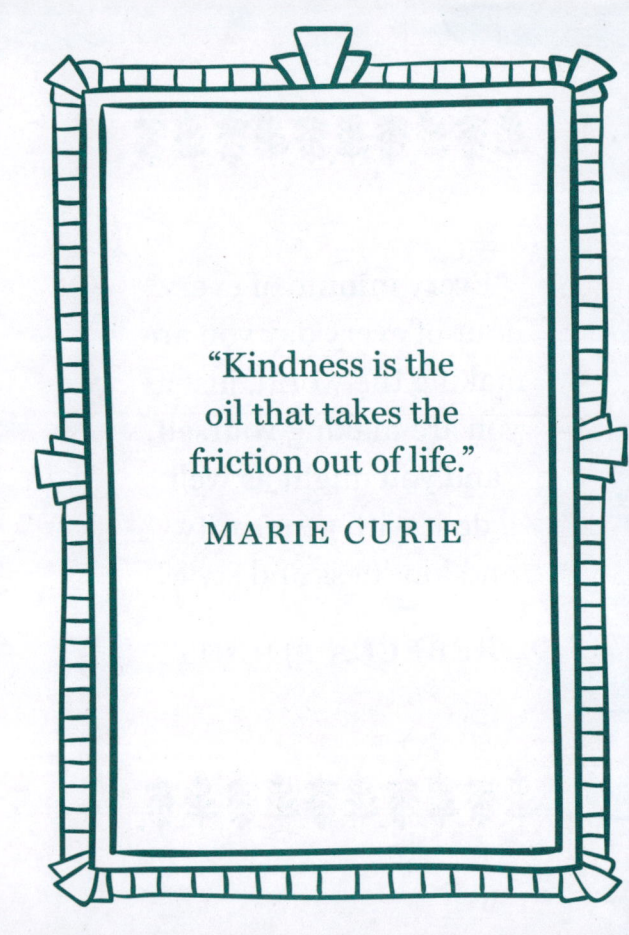

"Kindness is the
oil that takes the
friction out of life."

MARIE CURIE

"Kindness is the greatest wisdom."

ANONYMOUS

"The man who practises unselfishness, who is genuinely interested in the welfare of others, who feels it a privilege to have the power to do a fellow-creature a kindness—even though polished manners and a gracious presence may be absent—will be an elevating influence wherever he goes."

ORISON SWETT MARDEN

"There's nothing so kingly
as kindness, and nothing
so royal as truth."

ALICE CARY

"Always be kind, but kindness
doesn't mean that you have
to not say what you think."

GRACE VANDERWAAL

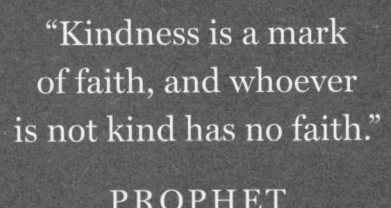

"Kindness is a mark
of faith, and whoever
is not kind has no faith."

PROPHET
MUHAMMAD

"The everyday kindness of the back roads more than makes up for the acts of greed in the headlines."

CHARLES KURALT

"REMEMBER THAT
EVERYONE YOU MEET IS
AFRAID OF SOMETHING,
LOVES SOMETHING, AND
HAS LOST SOMETHING."

H. Jackson Brown Jr.

"No one has yet realized the wealth of sympathy, the kindness and generosity hidden in the soul of a child. The effort of every true education should be to unlock that treasure."

EMMA GOLDMAN

"I guess at the end of the
day, all women like to be
appreciated and treated
with respect and kindness."

SOFIA VERGARA

"It is impossible to treat a child too well. Children are spoiled by being ignored too much or by harshness, not by kindness."

SLOAN WILSON

"Try to exercise gentleness, kindness and humour, and you cannot go far wrong."

SOPHIE WINKLEMAN

"THE BEST WAY TO FIND YOURSELF IS TO LOSE YOURSELF IN THE SERVICE OF OTHERS."

Mahatma Gandhi

"And as I've gotten older, I've had more of a tendency to look for people who live by kindness, tolerance, compassion, a gentler way of looking at things."

MARTIN SCORSESE

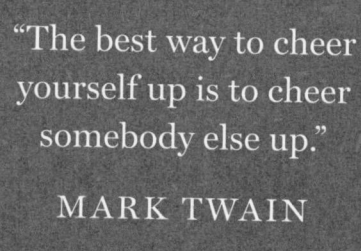

"The best way to cheer
yourself up is to cheer
somebody else up."

MARK TWAIN

"THE GREATEST GIFT YOU
CAN GIVE SOMEONE IS YOUR
KINDNESS AND ATTENTION."

Debasish Mridha

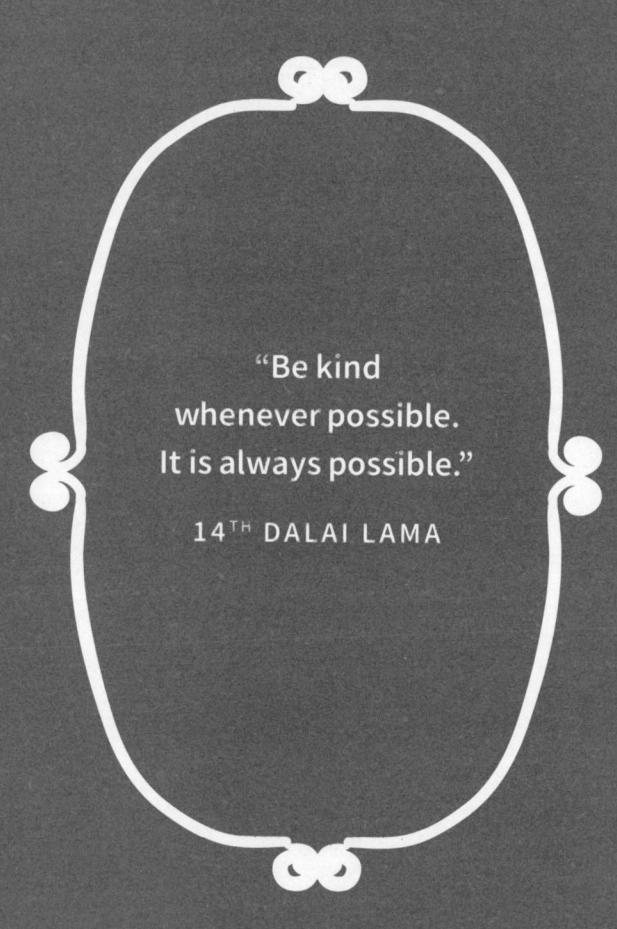

"Be kind
whenever possible.
It is always possible."

14TH DALAI LAMA

"One who knows how
to show and to accept
kindness will be a friend
better than any possession."

SOPHOCLES

"Kindness is the golden
chain by which society
is bound together."

JOHANN WOLFGANG
VON GOETHE

"My philosophy is that the most important aspect of any religion should be human kindness. And to try to ease the suffering of others. To try to bring light and love into the lives of mankind."

STEVEN SEAGAL

"Kindness is a powerful force.
It can heal wounds,
mend broken relationships,
and bring peace
to troubled hearts."

ANONYMOUS

"We rise by lifting others."

ROBERT GREEN
INGERSOLL

"I HAVE ALWAYS
DEPENDED ON
THE KINDNESS
OF STRANGERS."

Tennessee Williams

"He that has done you a kindness will be more ready to do you another, than he whom you yourself have obliged."

BENJAMIN FRANKLIN

"I feel no need for any other faith than my faith in the kindness of human beings. I am so absorbed in the wonder of earth and the life upon it that I cannot think of heaven and angels."

PEARL S. BUCK

"True popularity comes
from acts of kindness rather
than acts of stupidity."

BO BENNETT

"I AM NOT A PRODUCT OF MY CIRCUMSTANCES. I AM A PRODUCT OF MY DECISIONS."

Stephen R. Covey

"Kindness and a generous spirit go a long way. And a sense of humor. It's like medicine—very healing."

MAX IRONS

"I don't want to say everything happens for a reason but every day is lined up right next to the other one for a reason. The best you can do is do each day well with kindness and as a good person."

MAYIM BIALIK